…'s Lodging

…Stirling

Richard Fawcett

CONTENTS *Page*

EDITED BY CHRIS TABRAHAM
ILLUSTRATED BY DAVID SIMON
PHOTOGRAPHY BY HISTORIC SCOTLAND PHOTOGRAPHIC UNIT
PRODUCED BY ROY STEWART PRINT SERVICES
PRINTED IN SCOTLAND BY BUCCLEUCH PRINTERS LTD., HAWICK

FIRST PUBLISHED BY HISTORIC SCOTLAND 1996
REPRINTED 1999

ISBN 1 900168 08 1

Introduction

"And the said david McBeath is to enter and beginn to the foresaid works the threttiethe day of Aprile instant and he binds and oblidgs him to finish and compleit the foresaid haill work (lyfe and health permitting)."

(Part of the Contract agreed in 1675 between Archibald Campbell, Ninth Earl of Argyll, and David McBeath, artist, for works associated with the refurbishment of Argyll's Lodging)

Argyll's Lodging, the residence of the Earls (later the Dukes) of Argyll in Stirling, is the finest and most complete surviving example in Scotland of a seventeenth-century town residence. Set back behind a screen wall on the upper approaches to Stirling Castle, its fine architecture marks it out as a town house intended for the household of a great nobleman serving the royal court within the castle. In fact, by the time it was built, Scotland's Stewart Kings were also Kings of England, and were seldom able to make 'hamecomings' to their northern kingdom, though the two main phases of the house's construction correspond to periods when royal visits to Scotland looked likely to become more frequent.

As now seen, composed of three ranges around a delightfully enclosed courtyard with conically-roofed stair turrets at the angles, Argyll's Lodging has something of the feeling of a French provincial town house. However, its air of timeless architectural unity conceals a more complex structural history. Hidden within one corner are the remains of

Archibald Campbell, ninth Earl of Argyll, arrives at his lodging in 1680; an artist's impression.

a much smaller building ~ probably sixteenth-century ~ which was later enlarged into the sort of tower house that was widespread in Scotland. But most of what is now seen dates from two major phases of enlargement in the 1630s and 1670s, the first carried out for the first Earl of Stirling, and the second for the ninth Earl of Argyll. After 1800 the house served a number of uses, including a military hospital and a youth hostel.

Argyll's Lodging and its Owners

THE GREAT HOUSES OF STIRLING

The land-holding magnates who played a leading part in the government of medieval and Renaissance Scotland, and who depended on royal favour for their continued prosperity, were expected to spend part of their time at court, and thus found themselves following the King around the castles, palaces and monasteries in which he chose to reside. From at least the early twelfth century one of the most important of these residences was Stirling Castle. When the King was in residence some of his principal courtiers were accommodated within the castle; others had to find lodging within the burgh. However, as ideas of what was fitting for a nobleman expanded, many came to see the attraction of building a house of their own within the burgh.

The main approach to Stirling Castle from the burgh passed through the market place, now known as Broad Street. This area, and the roads around it, came to be flanked by many fine houses of the nobility who served the court or had estates near Stirling, and of the wealthier burgesses of the town. The most imposing of these, Mar's Wark, which still dominates the upper end of Broad Street, was started in 1570 for the Earl of Mar, who became Regent in 1571. However, his death within the castle in 1572 meant that little more than the entrance range was completed.

Other houses were built along Castle Wynd, where the road turned from the market to go up to the castle; the Earls of Argyll, who owned various tenements within Stirling from at least the fourteenth century, appear to have had land at this corner by the sixteenth century. The land beyond the corner, where Argyll's Lodging now stands, was acquired in 1629 by Sir William Alexander, who was soon afterwards created first Earl of Stirling, and whose family was closely connected with the Earls of Argyll. Fragments of earlier work within the north-east corner of Argyll's Lodging show there was already a substantial house here at that time, perhaps dating from the later sixteenth century.

It is difficult to be certain from the complex records of land-ownership within Stirling who may have built that house, though it seems likely that it was Adam Erskine, Commendator of Cambuskenneth Abbey. He is recorded as resigning a "*new and great house or manor*" to another member of his family, Sir James Erskine of Craig, in 1604. This may have been the same tenement which had been conveyed in 1559 to Adam Erskine's servant by John Traill, a burgess of St Andrews, and which was apparently eventually conveyed by the Erskines to the future Earl of Stirling. Lord Stirling's wife, Janet, incidentally was a member of a cadet branch of the Erskine family.

Mar's Wark, at the upper end of Broad Street, begun by the Regent Mar in 1570.

The First Earl of Stirling

Sir William Alexander was probably born at Menstrie, north-east of Stirling, in 1577. Menstrie had been held by the family since around the early sixteenth century from the Earls of Argyll, whose own main Lowland estates were also in this area. After his father's death in 1581, he was brought up by a great-uncle, a burgess of Stirling, who sent him to the University of Glasgow, and perhaps later to that of Leiden. He became a prolific poet, and eventually befriended Ben Johnson and William Drummond of Hawthornden.

William also became a particularly colourful character at the courts of James VI and Charles I. He had been fortunate to be invited to accompany the seventh Earl of Argyll on his travels through France, Italy and Spain, and it may have been Argyll who introduced him at the court of James VI. There he was appointed tutor to the heir to the throne, Prince Henry. In 1603 King James moved to London after succeeding to the English throne, and Alexander soon followed, having been appointed one of the gentlemen extraordinary to Prince Henry's Private Chamber. He received a knighthood in 1609. He was made Master of Requests in 1614, and Secretary for Scotland in 1626. In 1630 he was created Viscount Stirling and Lord Alexander of Tullibody, and in 1631 was made an extraordinary Judge of the Court of Session.

Sir William Alexander, Earl of Stirling. Much of his life was devoted to dreaming up money-making schemes. In 1608 he was granted the right to collect unpaid taxes in England. In 1613 he was working silver mines at Crawford Muir and Hilderston. Another scheme was the issuing of copper two-pence pieces to the value of £100,000 Scots, as one way for Charles I to pay off his debts to Alexander; but the coins, or 'black turners' were widely regarded as worthless. His greatest ploy was the attempted colonisation of Nova Scotia following a grant of the territory in 1621. Alexander sold 6000-acre parcels of land, along with the honour of a baronetcy. The scheme eventually lost royal support and collapsed.

Menstrie Castle, north-east of Stirling, Sir William Alexander's ancestral seat. It has been restored by the National Trust for Scotland, and is now divided into a number of smaller houses.

Sir William acquired the nucleus of his new house in Stirling in 1629. For some years Charles I had been promising to visit Scotland, and there were real hopes that there would once again be a regular royal presence in the northern kingdom. In 1633, when the King eventually returned home for his Scottish coronation, major works were carried out on Alexander's new house, and he was further ennobled with the titles of Earl of Stirling and Viscount Canada. Six years later he was also granted the earldom of Dovan. Despite all this, he died insolvent in 1640, and left his family in severe financial difficulty.

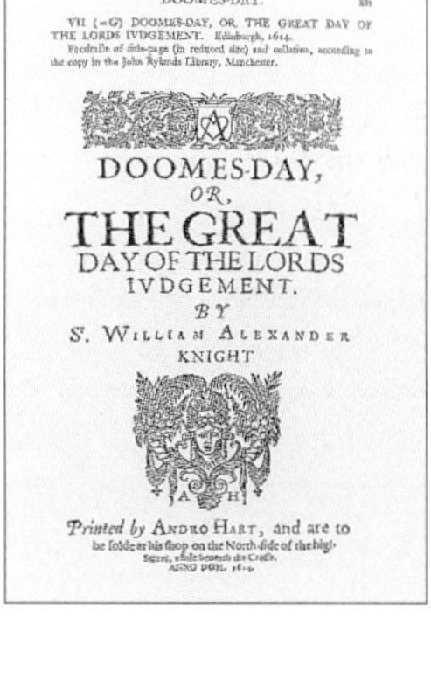

DOOMES-DAY. xli

VII (=G) DOOMES-DAY, OR, THE GREAT DAY OF THE LORDS IVDGEMENT. Edinburgh, 1614.

Facsimile of title-page (in reduced size) and collation, according to the copy in the John Rylands Library, Manchester.

DOOMES-DAY,
OR,
THE GREAT
DAY OF THE LORDS
IVDGEMENT.
BY
S^r. William Alexander
KNIGHT

A H

Printed by Andro Hart, and are to be solde at his shop on the North-side of the high-Street, a little beneath the Crosse.
ANNO DOM. 1614.

The title-page of Doomes-day, *by Sir William Alexander. Many of his poems were written on royal themes, including the tragedy of* Darius, *a sequence of love sonnets called* Aurora, *and* A Paraenesis to the Prince *which dared to suggest that unjust rulers might be deposed. Most of his works will strike the modern reader as rather ponderous, especially* Doomes-day, *a vast epic eventually expanded into 12 books, but in their day they were highly thought of, and Drummond of Hawthornden considered Alexander's love poetry to be as good as Shakespeare's.*

THE NINTH EARL OF ARGYLL

At his death Lord Stirling's rights in his Stirling town house passed to his fifth son, Charles, but the town council soon foreclosed on a mortgage they held on the property. For a while there were plans to make it into an almshouse. These were abandoned in the 1660s when it was agreed to sell the house to the Earl of Argyll, whose family may have already owned the adjoining property. The earliest reference in the burgh records to the Earl's connection with the new lodging was in 1664, when he complained that a boundary had been moved. But it was only in the following year that he agreed to pay £1000 for the house, four years hence, and in fact payment was long delayed. It was eventually disponed to him on 16 May 1668. In 1674 Argyll granted the house to his second wife, Anna Mackenzie, a daughter of the Earl of Seaforth, as part of her jointure at a time when he was engaged in major rebuilding.

Castle Campbell, near Dollar, the Lowland residence of the Earls of Argyll. Inveraray Castle, in Argyllshire, was their chief seat.

Archibald Campbell, ninth Earl of Argyll, was born in 1629, the son of the Marquess of Argyll, who is best remembered for his Covenanting sympathies and his conflict with the royalist Marquess of Montrose. Despite carrying the crown at Charles II's coronation in 1651, the Marquess of Argyll became a supporter of Cromwell's Commonwealth, for which he paid with his life in 1661 after King Charles had returned to his throne. His son, however, was more strongly royalist and succeeded in having the family estates restored to him in 1663, together with the earldom but not the marquessate. Argyll became a close ally of the Secretary for Scotland, the Duke of Lauderdale, and his son, also Archibald, married Lauderdale's step-daughter. Lauderdale was particularly anxious to increase the royal presence in Scotland, and made great efforts to persuade Charles II to rebuild his palace at Holyrood, in Edinburgh. In fact the King, who had unhappy memories from his Scottish coronation, probably had no intention of returning to Scotland, but the possibility of royal visits perhaps influenced Argyll's decision to extend his new town house in Stirling in 1674.

If Lauderdale was an ally, another powerful figure, the King's brother and heir presumptive, James Duke of Albany and York, was less favourable towards Argyll. In 1681 York was sent north as High Commissioner to the Scottish parliament, largely to get him out of England where his open Catholicism was creating difficulties. Argyll carried the crown at that parliament. York became concerned about Argyll's power in the west of Scotland and was also unsympathetic towards his markedly Protestant faith. Nevertheless, the two had to work together, and York visited Argyll at his Stirling house during his stay. However, the turning-point in Argyll's life was the Test Act of that same year, which required all people of standing to swear acceptance of royal authority and to renounce the Covenants. Argyll said he was only prepared to take the oath so far as it was consistent within itself. This was deemed treasonable and he was imprisoned in Edinburgh Castle and sentenced to death. He escaped dressed as his step-daughter's page and fled to Holland. When King Charles died and York became James VII and II in 1685, Argyll was persuaded to lead a rebellion in Scotland, to coincide with the Duke of Monmouth's rising in England. But he was captured at Inchinnan, in Renfrewshire, in June and summarily beheaded under the sentence passed on him in 1681.

The laigh, or lower, hall, on the ground floor of Argyll's Lodging as it might have looked after the Earl of Argyll's alterations.

THE LATER HISTORY OF ARGYLL'S LODGING

The house remained in the ownership of the Argyll family for over a century, and further work was carried out in 1706 when payments were made on behalf of the second Duke to Adam Jack, slater, John Ferguson, smith, and Alexander Howie, glazier. The Duke of Cumberland stayed in the house in 1746 during his campaign to crush the Jacobite Rising.

Castle Wynd in the early nineteenth century, with the entrance to Argyll's Lodging on the left. At this date the Lodging was being used as a military hospital for the castle garrison and the west range adjacent to the street was still standing.

The house was sold by the fourth Duke of Argyll in 1764, and for a short period was owned jointly by Robert Campbell and James Wright, who then sold it to the McGregors of Balhaldie. Around 1800 they sold it to the Crown, after which it was used as a military hospital serving the castle garrison. During this period, part of the late-seventeenth-century west range along the street was demolished.

After Stirling Castle ceased to be a military depot in 1964, the house became a youth hostel. In 1996 Historic Scotland opened the main rooms to visitors, using replica furniture and furnishings to display them as they may have appeared at the time they were lived in by the ninth Earl of Argyll.

Argyll's Lodging shortly before it passed out of Army use in 1964.

A Short Tour o

Please note that parts of Argyll's Lodging are not normally accessible to visitors.

1. Courtyard

Visitors see the house much as it would have looked in the 1670s, following remodelling by the Ninth Earl of Argyll. The only major loss since then has been part of a range along the street frontage. The earliest parts, dating to the later sixteenth century, are in the north-east corner and north wing [5].

2. Laigh Hall

The lower of two reception rooms in the Earl of Stirling's house (c.1630s) which perhaps also served as a dining room for the Earl of Argyll's senior attendants in the 1670s. Original features include the fireplace and the buffet recess. The balustraded stair of scale- and platt- (straight flight and landing) type is probably a replacement from the 1670s.

3. High Dining Room

The most important reception room of the house. Notable elements from the 1630s include the fireplace and the buffet recess (where the family plate was displayed). A particularly fine feature is the wall decoration, painted by David McBeath in 1675.

Argyll's Lodging

4. State Apartment

THE PRINCIPAL SUITE OF ROOMS OF THE HOUSE IN THE 1670s. THE APARTMENT CONSISTED OF A SEQUENCE OF THREE ROOMS: AN OUTER CHAMBER OR DRAWING ROOM, LADY ARGYLL'S CLOSET, AND LORD AND LADY ARGYLL'S BED CHAMBER. THE FINE FIREPLACE IN THE DRAWING ROOM DATES FROM THE 1630s AND HAS TRACES OF THE PAINTED ARMS OF THE EARL OF STIRLING AND HIS LADY. BESIDE IT IS A BLOCKED DOORWAY WHICH PERHAPS GAVE ACCESS VIA A GALLERY TO THE GARDENS [6]. OPENING OFF THE BED CHAMBER IS A STOOL CLOSET (FOR A BOXED CHAMBER POT).

5. Kitchens and Offices

THE EARLIEST SURVIVING PARTS OF THE HOUSE, DATING TO THE 16TH CENTURY. THE SMALL KITCHEN AND TWO SMALL VAULTED ROOMS CONNECTED BY A CORRIDOR AT THE EAST END OF THE RANGE BELONG TO THE FIRST HOUSE. THE LARGER KITCHEN AT THE WEST END BELONGS TO ADDITIONS MADE LATER IN THE CENTURY.

6. Gardens

EXTENSIVE FORMAL GARDENS ONCE EXISTED HERE, LAID OUT IN THE SEVENTEENTH CENTURY, POSSIBLY BY THE NINTH EARL OF ARGYLL WHO WAS A KEEN GARDENER. THE GARDENS COULD PERHAPS BE REACHED DIRECTLY FROM THE EARL'S OUTER CHAMBER IN THE STATE APARTMENT [4].

Artist's bird's-eye view of Argyll's Lodging from the north west.

A Noble Town House

The Earliest Buildings

The earliest identifiable part of the building is at the north-east corner, where there are remains of a basically **rectangular house**, probably originally of two storeys and likely to date from the sixteenth century. The stone-vaulted **ground floor** has a **kitchen** at its east end, and two **cellars** interconnected by a corridor. The main feature of the kitchen is an arched fireplace, with a domed bread oven to one side. A blocked window on the right-hand side of the fireplace shows this was originally an outside wall. The upper floor of this building, of which only part of the west gable has been identified, embedded in later masonry, probably had a hall and chamber as accommodation for the owner, who may have been John Traill of St Andrews.

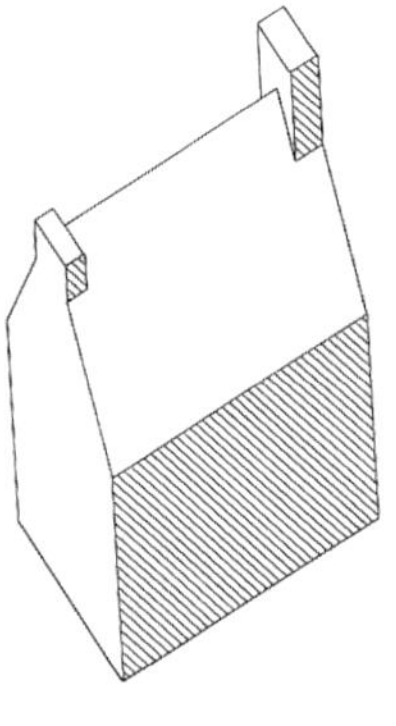

The earliest part of the building, was a rectangular house at the north-east corner.

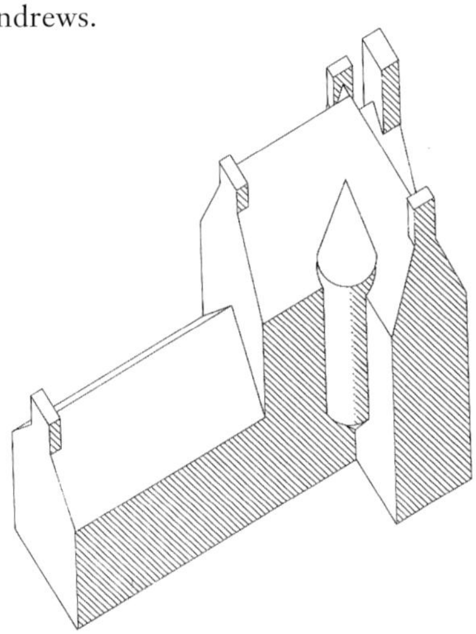

The rectangular house was converted into an L-shaped tower house with a kitchen wing later added to its west.

Later in the sixteenth century two additional storeys were added as well as a wing at the south-east corner, so giving it the form of an **L-shaped tower house**. This was probably the work of Adam Erskine. By analogy with other houses of this type, access to the first floor was probably by a spacious stair in the wing. Access above that level was by a spiral stair corbelled out in the angle between the two parts, which still survives.

The upper parts of the wing above the main stair would have contained additional chambers. Much of this building is still identifiable on the flank and garden front of the house because of its higher roofline, and from the simple rounded or chamfered surrounds of the windows. Its finest rooms were on the remodelled **first floor**, where there was a **hall**, with a projecting oriel window at the dais end, beyond which was a **bedchamber** with a stool closet off it.

A house like this had ancillary accommodation within an enclosed courtyard. The kitchens on the ground floor of the original house would have been inadequate for the enlarged building, and at some stage a **west wing** was added to provide a larger vaulted **kitchen and other offices**, and probably an upper floor lit by dormer windows. This seems to have been the extent of the house acquired by Lord Stirling around 1629.

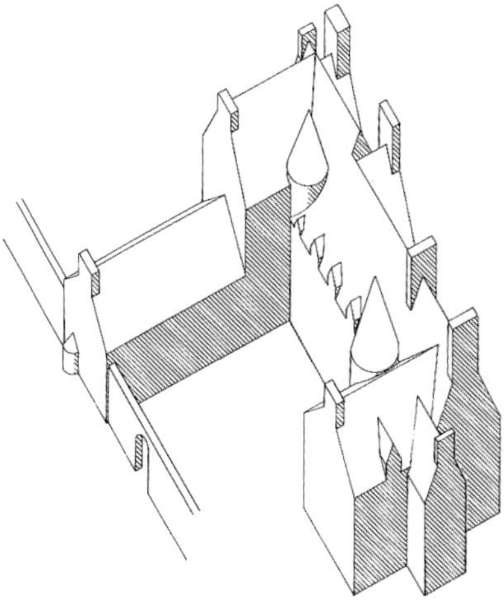

The extent of the first Earl of Stirling's residence.

THE ADDITIONS FOR THE FIRST EARL OF STIRLING

Soon after purchasing the house, Lord Stirling set about greatly enlarging it. An imposing **new range** containing the principal rooms ran southwards from the wing of the existing house, and was extended at its southern end by a short **wing** which balanced the main body of the earlier house. The resulting plan formed a shallow west-facing C, with the hollow towards the **courtyard**, around parts of which were lower buildings. The screen wall across the west side of the courtyard was probably also built at this time, though it was later modified.

As usual at this period, the **main rooms** were at **first-floor level**. The central part was taken up by what was later known as the **high dining room** (perhaps to distinguish it from the **laigh (lower) hall** below). Beyond the high dining room are likely to have been an **outer and inner chamber** (known by the 1680s as a drawing room and bedchamber) with a **closet** between them in the off-shoot on the south side of the building. Together these rooms were probably intended as a **state apartment**, perhaps normally occupied by Lord Stirling himself, but given over to guests of higher status when the occasion demanded. Since no inventories from before 1680 survive we cannot be certain of the precise use of the rooms at this time but there was probably some flexibility of use.

The main access to the first floor is by a handsome timber **balustraded stair** which rises around three sides of a stairwell at the north end of the laigh hall, though the present stair may date from the 1670s. There was also access between the floors by way of a projecting spiral stair at the south end of the courtyard. Another apartment was provided on the ground floor below the state apartment, and there were further apartments on the first and second floors.

The internal decoration was of the highest quality. The best surviving fireplaces are those in the high dining room and drawing room. The lintel of the dining room fireplace is supported by a male and female figure on pedestals. That in the drawing room is carried on mythical beasts with human heads and lions' paws. Extensive traces of painted decoration have been found on both fireplaces, that on the second fireplace including the arms of the Earl of Stirling and his wife, Janet Erskine.

The fireplace in the drawing room.

Externally the house was lavishly adorned; even the bases of the chimney stacks were elaborated with volutes (scrolls). The angles of the buildings have buckle-shaped quoins, a common motif found on many fine buildings of the period. The quoins on the south side of the courtyard provide the clearest external evidence for the extent of that range in the 1630s. The greatest architectural emphasis was concentrated on the **main entrance**, which is surmounted by Lord Stirling's coat of arms. The doorway itself is now covered by a porch, with the date 1632 in its gablet. This porch does not fit its present position very well and was clearly made for elsewhere. It may have been resited here in the 1670s.

The main entrance facade.

The windows towards the courtyard were capped by elaborate strapwork gablets, with particular prominence given to those on the second floor, which rise above the eaves cornice as dormers. At the rear of the house, only the window directly above the garden doorway and the dormer windows seem to have been treated as elaborately. At this time only the upper parts of the main windows were glazed; internally there would have been two levels of shutters. All the windows now have later sashes.

Whoever designed Lord Stirling's work was a master mason of high calibre. Stirling's second son, Anthony, had been appointed joint royal master of works in 1629, but we know very little about any buildings with which he may have been involved. Since it is unclear whether he was an architect himself, it seems he may not have been the designer of his father's house. The architectural details show close analogies with major buildings of the period, such as George Heriot's Hospital, in Edinburgh. One possible designer might be William Ayton, in charge of Heriot's from 1631; another could be John Mylne, who became royal master mason in 1636. Both were later involved in the building of Cowane's Hospital in Stirling.

The fine balustraded main stair.

The Extensions for the Ninth Earl of Argyll

The modifications carried out for the ninth Earl of Argyll appear to have involved the heightening of the north wing and the **addition** or remodelling of a **T-shaped block** at the **western end of the south wing**. This completed the enclosure of the south side of the courtyard and extended into a range running along Castle Wynd. Much of this range was demolished in the nineteenth century (see the illustration on page 10) but it possibly incorporated part of the earlier residence of the Earls of Argyll, on the land adjacent to Lord Stirling's. A bill of 1675 by John McPharlane, slater, refers to work on both old and new lodgings, suggesting they were connected in some way.

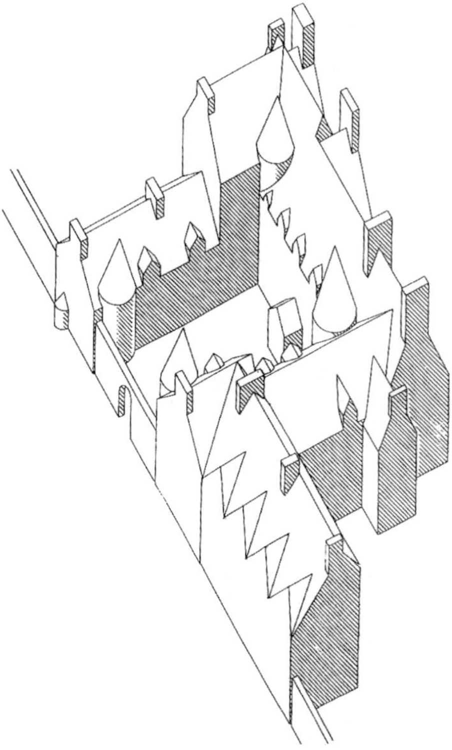

The extent of the Earl of Argyll's lodging.

The only other accounts surviving from this period are for plastering and painting in the high dining room (see the reconstruction on page 23). The painting was carried out by the Edinburgh artist David McBeath. A contract of 7 April 1675 specified that 19 Corinthian pillars were to be painted; McBeath sought payment for this in January 1676. His work is best preserved on the wooden partition separating the room from the stair, where the painted Corinthian pilasters above a dado survive remarkably complete. Decorative unity was given to the room by the way the painted frieze reflects the carved decoration on the fireplace frieze. Along the edges of the ceiling the cornice has small painted modillions (brackets). This decorative scheme has now been restored above a layer of lining paper which protects the traces of the original. Original work can be seen in its conserved state on the timber partition.

Detail of a Corinthian pilaster, one of 19 painted by David McBeath in 1675. These painted pilasters were closely based on the pilasters on the inner face of the courtyard screen wall.

The details of the Earl's additions are more restrained than those of Lord Stirling's. The **outer gate** to the courtyard screen wall is probably of this period, and has Tuscan pilasters flanking an arch, all massively rusticated. The windows and doorways are capped by pediments of segmental or concave triangular form, some bearing an earl's coronet and the boar's head crest of the Argylls; one doorway pediment is dated 1674. Yet the division between Lord Stirling's and Argyll's work is not as straightforward as might first seem. The window pediments on the first floor of the north wing are identical to those on Argyll's south wing but they bear the initials of the Earl and Countess of Stirling. The doorway at the base of the stair turret at the outer end of that wing, which is identical to the turret of the outer end of the south wing dated 1674, has traces of the date 1633. However, it seems unlikely that the upper floors and stair turret of the north wing in their present form were part of Lord Stirling's work, particularly since the only traces of fixed upper glazing such as we saw in his work elsewhere are on the lintels, which appear re-used. Although we cannot be sure, it seems that Argyll was recording his own contribution along one side of the courtyard, and that of his predecessor along the other. This seems all the more likely given the close connections between the two families.

The outer gate, with the main entrance into the lodging beyond. The design of the gate was partly inspired by an engraving in a book by Alessandro Francini, first published in 1631 but which only became available in English in 1669.

Argyll's house must have functioned essentially as an expanded version of that provided for Lord Stirling. **Kitchens and other offices** were still on the **ground floor of the north wing**, and the main core of **public rooms** were at the **centre of the east range**. As before, the **state apartment** led off the far end of the high dining room, now entered by a more imposing doorway with the Earl's painted initials and coronet in its pediment. But now there was presumably also accommodation for other members of the Earl's family in the expanded south wing. Around all of this was an array of other apartments and individual bedchambers. Two inventories, taken in 1680 and 1682 when the house was settled on the Earl's second wife, help our understanding of the functioning of the house, although we cannot be entirely certain of the sequence in which the rooms are listed.

Vertical communication within the house was by means of no less than **six sets of stairs** - the main stair between ground and first floor, the two spiral stairs at the inner angles of the courtyard, two additional spiral stairs in the octagonal turrets at the outer angles of the courtyard, and a further spiral stair behind the street range. This made it possible to have separate access to each apartment. In addition, a blocked doorway on one side of the fireplace in the Earl's outer chamber indicates that there was direct access to the **gardens**; traces of supports for a gallery at this point have been seen beneath the external harling. Argyll was a keen gardener and eighteenth-century maps show that the house by then had extensive formal gardens.

The Earl's and Countess's bedchamber as it might have looked in the 1680s.

THE HOUSE TODAY

Some of the principal rooms have now been refurnished as they might have appeared around 1680 during the ninth Earl of Argyll's occupation. The **laigh hall** on the ground floor, which perhaps also served as a dining room for the Earl's more senior attendants, is shown with a dining table; in a side wall is a buffet recess (see the reconstruction on page 9). The laigh hall may have been separated from the stair by a screen, but since we have no idea what form this took it has not been restored.

At the head of the main stair, on the first floor, is the richly-decorated **high dining room**. This was the principal reception room where the Earl met and entertained important guests on formal occasions. The furniture, consisting mainly of folding tables and chairs, was placed around the walls when not required.

Beyond the high dining room was the first room of the 'state apartment', the **drawing room**. This was the Earl's main 'living room', where he conversed with his more

The high dining room as it might have looked in the 1680s.

favoured guests, and also dined on more intimate occasions. Although smaller than the high dining room, it was more richly furnished, with Arras tapestries hanging from the walls. There was a canopied day bed here in 1680, though this had been replaced with a chair of state by 1682. The **closet** off the drawing room was used by the Countess and contained many of her personal belongings, including her husband's portrait.

The Earl and Countess's **bedchamber** was dominated by their great bed, often the most expensive single item of furniture in an aristocratic household; theirs had purple hangings matching those on the walls (see the reconstruction on page 22). This was the most private room of the apartment, though more people had access to it than we might imagine, and the Earl may have received certain favoured guests while sitting up in the bed, a sign of aristocratic condescension. A doorway at the far end of the room led through to other family rooms. Other doorways opened into the stool closet and onto the spiral stair used by the servants to gain access to the apartment without their having to pass through the more public areas. Some of these doorways may have been fitted with fixed timber draught screens, though by the 1680s there were movable screens covered with the same purple cloth as on the walls and bed.

Further Reading

ON THE LODGING:

J Ronald *The Story of the Argyle Lodging* (1906)

Royal Commission on the Ancient and Historical Monuments of Scotland *Inventory of Stirlingshire*, vol.2 (1963)

C McKean *Stirling and the Trossachs* (1985)

R Fawcett *Stirling Castle* (1996)

ON THE FAMILIES:

A Lindsay *A Memoir of Lady Anna Mackenzie* (1868)

J Willcock *A Scots Earl: The Life and Times of Archibald Ninth Earl of Argyll* (1907)

T McGrail *Sir William Alexander, First Earl of Stirling* (1940)